MW01658130

THIS DISEASE

Thanks!

THIS DISEASE

POEMS BY

BARRY SILESKY

UNIVERSITY OF TAMPA PRESS • TAMPA, FLORIDA

Copyright © 2006 by Barry Silesky. All rights reserved.

Manufactured in the United States of America
Printed on acid-free paper ∞
First Edition

No part of this book may be reproduced, stored in a retrieval system, or transmitted in any form or by any means, electronic, mechanical, photocopying, recording, or otherwise, except as may be expressly permitted by the applicable copyright statutes or in writing by the publisher.

The University of Tampa Press
401 West Kennedy Boulevard
Tampa, FL 33606

ISBN-13 978-1-59732-016-1 (hbk) ISBN-10 1-59732-016-1 (hbk)
ISBN-13 978-59732-017-7 (pbk) ISBN-10 1-59732-017-X (pbk.)

Browse & order online at
http://utpress.ut.edu

Library of Congress Cataloging-in-Publication Data

Silesky, Barry, 1949-
This disease : poems / by Barry Silesky.
p. cm.
ISBN-13: 978-1-59732-016-0 (acid-free paper) ISBN-10: 1-59732-016-1 (acid-free paper)
ISBN-13: 978-1-59732-017-7 (pbk. : acid-free paper) ISBN-10: 1-59732-017-X (pbk. : acid-free paper)
I. Title.

PS3569.I4214T48 2006
811'.54--dc22 2006025831

For Sharon, For Seth, For Jesse

CONTENTS

I. THE SYSTEM

II. SPRING TRAINING

III. NATURE

I. THE SYSTEM

Archeology

Holiday snow quiets the whole neighborhood and music opens the pores. For once the hormones are at rest. Okay, not really, but now I can slump in front of the TV, watch the aliens explode. Tonight, there is no other street. The magic? Unemployment at twenty-five year low. Magnets relieve muscle pain. Then eat this: A little sour, maybe, but isn't that the point—an echo of the ripe apples, the egret stalking the edge of the dump, purple blossoms lining the dirt road in the painting. Streaks of orange, red, white play amid shadows. If we look too closely the whole thing comes apart, but we're not going to. Let the phone ring. We're walking as far as we can see, past the pig slumping in the ditch, the vultures perched in that tree. Under the mounds of dirt behind the trees, the ancient ruins wait to be discovered.

To You

Dear Sarah, I always loved the name. Or Elizabeth,
for all the variations, elegance and privilege

beyond my tribe. Queen for Every Day,
I have to see pores and membranes, parts

that seem disgusting, until we steel ourselves,
learn by repetition. My job is to clean

the bathroom, wade in dirt I'm used to,
sensations, odors that couldn't be

her, they say from their distance. But here
she is, closer than that, and I'm buried in

mucous and stench. She's laughing, she's
coming at me, holding out the pail, muck

splashing over the brim, and I can't
leave it alone. But no, I'm wrong again—

she doesn't care at all. The desire bubbles
up from my own remains, re-forms,

scatters, and I can barely hear the voice.
Sorry, I never liked those show tunes that

send me back to the family I keep
trying to leave. Still, they're all I hear.

If I've got the name wrong again, I've got to
believe she'll forgive me. She knows

what I need. It's a hundred degrees, and
the air conditioner's broken.

The House of Her

"He who does not accept this world builds no house here"
–Henri Michaux

Depending what's meant by house. Depending
what's meant by here. Winter, for instance,
descends with the usual white. A day later it rains,

the snow's gone, it's cold, then it's not.
Or it's the alley across from the stadium, lined with
garbage cans, brick buildings millions pass every summer.

Years of collecting, and none have brought me
the nods of "in charge," the yes
I've always wanted to this seeing. In the end,

the story contained in the words' arrangement
rises, calls: how many rooms have we made?
Maybe it isn't a house; it's all there is.

Call it beginning? Time to add the lover? The dream?
The one with black, red, long, short hair. The one
the one the one the one. I was burrowing up

from the cave where the people I loved
reclined at home. I was driving
alone on an empty street, steeper and

steeper, until the car stopped, pointing up.
Broken stone filled every direction.
I was scared. I woke. She was

never there. I don't think of her at all.

Box Seats

First, the wedding. Cute, aren't they? It's me, of course, despite her blue eyes, flowers, fashion I never managed. And we're on the way! Jamaica! Paris! Full of her brilliance, devotion to my every word, I love the sofa she chose for the den; the way she laughs when I drink myself dumb, drool at her girl friends. Of course the children don't listen, insisting the last word—But this great new tie! A dog with a basketball! Or is it red and gray dots? The war is horrible, but it's not our country. Those women flirting with me keep her attention. We love the new car, my hair thinning elegantly as her breasts fall. Okay, her father's right, the rows of carrots are ragged, the whole garden a bit shabby, but the grin's infectious. When the children break the antique chair, she's every right to lose her temper. Eventually we'll talk again. Meantime, the baseball stadium on the next block fills and empties, fills and empties. Just take me out to the ballgame, every day.

Bedtime Story

She's going out tonight, leaving the kids hungry. I find them half a banana, a dish of ice cream, and they're delighted to lean on my arm while I read the stories: robbery ring broken in north side apartment. Guerrillas pour over a southern border. Then a flicker of bare skin peeks from across the alley. She hasn't got a name; in fact, that woman doesn't exist. Others do, or did, but each is more distant every day. A ghost is coming, I tell the boys, it's scary, but their swords will protect them. They have to hold tight. Then they're tucked away and the night begins in earnest. The moaning at the door, the windows, must be wind. I'll check the locks, sharpen the saw. Set out the poison. Imagine her hair. Have a drink against the noise. It's another night twisting on the mattress to the music of violins. A scrap of cloth falls away, so close I think I can touch her. It must be a dream. It gets louder.

TREE OF HEAVEN

When I first came back to the city I wanted
to bring the chain saw. The scar
above my left knee, cut when a young oak fell
the wrong way in the woods I left was fresh,

and I can still see the torn
jeans, the gap the chain
opened as it leapt by into the snow.
I stared at the wound, breath

gone smoke as blood spilled over the space.
But I was afraid I might use it, set the engine
roaring against garbage trucks, el trains
screeching past the porch, drunks

splattering bottles in the alley. I swore
this was no place to live. Then every June
catalpa's white flowers, October
berries of mountain ash, gaudy reds and gold

of all those immigrant plants painting
buildings, parks, lakeshore remind us
we do. And there's more. The latest storm blows
out over the lake. Leaves turn, fall, come back.

Years later I brought the saw here to trim
mulberry and chinese elm in my new front yard.
The engine needed work, the chain sharpening,
it woke the babies, the neighbors stared.

But I loved the country it brought me, power
filling hands, arms, skin, blotting
airplanes, traffic, rock 'n roll screaming
from the apartment across the street.

Now let that scum who snuck in our yard
to steal my bike show his face, the one who clipped
our tulips in their finest bloom a night last May.
The one who beat the old woman down the block.

They grow like weeds, these ailanthus, these
"trees of heaven" that stink and spread everywhere,
their shade patches that won't cool
in some paradise no one believes. Roots thicken

under us, invisible ring by ring
until concrete and asphalt swell, buckle;
streets, walks, foundation walls lean and
break open. We've got to cut out those trees

before they do their damage. The one on the edge
of the walk scraped our window all winter, split
the short wall holding back the neighbors' yard.
I want room for a flowering crab, its obscene flush

painting a week so delicious I can almost
taste flesh, flower, spring; cherry, magnolia,
no matter what diseases those foreigners
might bring. Such May days feel

half the reason we live, and this year I'm going to
clear the junk, lose those extra pounds,
get to work. But I gave the saw away.
No time to keep the engine tuned, chain sharp

for the one day a year it might be used.
I took a bow saw up the ladder, balanced

in the first crotch, roped the bough to pull it
and cut the notch in front so it would fall

in our yard when I made the back cut.
Almost through, I stepped on the ladder, leaned
and held the other branch, sawed down.
And it worked: the familiar sweat and crack

as the bough broke off. Now the window's quiet
in the wind, but more than half that tree's
left, leaning over the deck next door.
The lower trunk's flush against the fence;

if I had the chain saw I could cut a notch,
work the tip into the back. I'd have to
be careful, fell it against its lean.
But that machine's long gone.

With only the bow saw, a ladder too short,
a little rope, I can't figure how
I'll get the rest of it down.
Last week someone sprayed a gang sign

on my back door. It looks like a fetus, blown up and
twisted beyond anything we can name.
This is my neighborhood, and I'm going to paint it
over, though I know they could be back any night.

They're everywhere. It looks like some version
of my initial. That scar on my knee's almost
gone now, but a month later a dozen new twigs
break from the old trunk. No saw can stop it.

Salvaged Wood

Gray blue ends of old boards shiver and steam.
Eight years collecting rain, snow blown
and melted; how long before they
sink back into the ground? I picked
at the streaked grain—it was my glasses—
a year old and already scratched. A wry smile
surrounds the view, mixed with the odor of obligation:
money gone. That pine could have been
porch walls, a lean-to. Instead, a souvenir spreads
in pieces from the morning we stacked them fresh,
to the inside walls that finally rose,
to the coast she left them for. What isn't rotted
might be kindling piled by the corner, more
than we'd use all winter, if it would still burn.
But no one lives here anymore. The leftover lumber,
rocks around the mock-orange and maple
are the children we never had, the last crumbs of sleep
the day won't admit as it pulls us
in, my presence stretched from here
to the city I live in, like the wires
the old woman in the madhouse novel swears tell her
secrets everyone keeps. But what are they?
And if I knew, would the geese settle, pigeons
retreat to themselves, leaving alone the broken
pump base attached to the pipe in that first well
halfway to the garden? It wasn't hard to fix;
the water was good there, so I drove the well
again. Too much pipe dope spoiled the taste.
Careless. Or just the old beyond recall?

*

Back in town, the doorbell rang and your ex-husband
stood there. For years he's been seven feet high,

muscles and black beard, slit of eyes
squinting into light. He made his land
from rock, bees swarm to gather his women, honey
piling through his hands as he works the hives.
And when we made love, it was him, his fingers
playing music my own stump over, his voice so sweet
mine's a horn in clogged traffic. He spoke and the rain
was gone, the earthquake a breeze in another life.
Except, he held a jar of honey, no beard at all,
but thin, tired, a wispy smile, a stranger
at a real door. His wife sat in the car.
Amazing how the house stood where it was.
Rotting wood forgotten, the room's prepared for
new furniture, and I've gone to get the scratched lens
repaired. Only two more names until it's my turn
to explain what I see—a man arguing on the phone,
a black haired woman with oversized frames
a technician's adjusting—the prescription I've taken
for granted fifteen years. I'm blinking, pushing
back my lenses, watching the woman
who's choosing. Are these new scratches on
the glass? Or scars on the table's surface
the polish highlights—antique distress, the current
fashion? Cleaning up that wood takes more than
minor adjustment; it was eight years getting there.
I order the repair and put on the old ones,
soldered where I broke them. They slide down
my nose as I run past bricks and boards, ideas
of that house, the lumber pile, blurred but unmistakable.
It's too old to burn, but it could be compost.
Next year, I swear, I'll take it an armload at a time
into the woods, leave it to work.

Thor's Helper

They're cutting out the stump now,
the saw's hum drifting
through city walls, carving
another world: cut oak
amid smells of pine, smoke
from the first fires. Split and stacked,

in a year the oak would be dried to warm us.
Enough for a few November days still
lies in back of the old house we built. Almost
deer season, long-necked geese swoop in and
out of the swamps, rough barks gather at sunset
on the way up, as the ragged V's

head out. Next week, the last trip north
to that house. I hauled the chimney
cement block by block to the roof, only
dropped the last eighty pound block near
the top. Made it all the way the second try.
Stood in snow waist deep to cut wood,

split out back stripped to a shirt in zero degrees.
I loved the sweat, the climb
to the roof to clean the chimney, check shingles,
any reason. Sharon and Joyce lay naked
on the deck below the day I vented the roof
the way I should have at first. I had to

build that deck twice. And once, shelves, each
wall, screen porch, every inch. It's not true
ash, that tree they're finishing off. It stood a long time.

Seventy feet high, four feet across, older
than four wars, six presidents, houses
on either side, this one.

"Thor's helper," from the rose family, the mountain ash
was said to ward off evil, pieces to stop
any disaster. We were going to live there
for good. So Clark drank too much,
talked too much the more he drank. So I fell in love
with Lynne, who lived with him,
and she half with me. So I drove the van
into a ditch after a long shot of whiskey
the night my wife left the message
she couldn't resist
that sailor. I can still see
the white snow in the headlights, my hands

clenched on the wheel. The house is finally
sold. Lynne married Dave. The wife
I had is gone. Dick and Denise
divorced. We planted
two birch, a white pine, vegetables, peonies, iris.
The bugs were impossible.

In the old countries, they'd carry twigs, splinters
of that ash for luck. It was another
age. I'd have tried it if I'd known. They're going to
build an apartment building in that yard.
Those winters would never end. Two hours,
and the tree's done.

County O

In a year, we were always there. Oak splits clean,
crackling as the snow piles, and here's another helping
of terrific homemade; isn't that the idea?
When I first tried it, the country collapsed
with a woman leaving, but now it's "free trade,"
a good job, and the old empire finally gone.
The kids love these woods, and the wife—

well, the wife. Of course she doesn't exist.
There are no kids. No more Golden Ox, City Lounge,
and the Other Woman, with her latest performance.
That therapist was something too, all the questions
muffled damage in a back room no one wants to discover,
until the door flies open, and the mess spreads over the floor.
Luckily, those days are gone. This must be the cleaning up.

The woman at the bar slips her fingers under his shirt,
and they're the couple he saw that night in the city—
not married, at least to each other, night dancing
as the weather wheels and blows on the other side
of the window. The food may not be as good out here,
but it's not so expensive either. They're kissing,
remember? She's not as pretty as his wife,

but the way she was there—and she was. Then the place
is closing, the highway home drifting over
until there's no getting through. Sure it's lonely at times;
isn't that the choice? The old team's star quits,
leaving the game to children, but there's woodsmoke,
deer, the raven's hoarse call. A new sport.
He's done oiling the works. He sights down the barrel.

The System

"Decentered phenomena combine a feeling that one knows the rules with the knowledge that one cannot predict the outcome." –Sherry Turkle

So things are warmer, which must explain the great blizzard, the disease stumbling him into another wall as the headlights freeze and bear down. With pieces everywhere, the weaving's too personal to understand; eyes glaze as the gorgeous pattern transfixes. Turn down those damn lights! Put another quarter in, sing along with that great dumb song. But the "meaning"? Whoever we are, in traces everywhere we look, lunch is surprisingly bland. Still, it did the job. Like the marriage arranged in the desert, ensuring the tribe—except we can't find the bones, and the ones in the cave that's finally uncovered simply don't belong. Such confusion as the species devolves—and yet, the very fact it's us offers comfort in the diffusion. Hey, it's not my fault. This desert was a sea, a place where the ancient tribes stored their stone mortars, bowls, pestles to grind seeds and corn. Then came the outlaws. There's the old muslin coat, Arioso coffee made with egg and sugar. On the left, there's the devil—we can tell by the horns—and elves, round heads polished for luck by thousands of hands who've come to see. They used to hold candles for light, climb dangerously, before the new century built this attraction. It's cool and deep. A little too late, maybe, for us to really enjoy the flesh, but it's what we've got. Outside it's a hundred degrees. We're diving in.

After The Body Deserts

(after Lucia Perillo)

The mind twirls about its post, shakes a limb, tries holding it still as the planets accelerate. As if the mind's another entity—not just a way of talking, which is a way of seeing: those two men for instance, standing in snow, mountains behind, pick-up truck stopped nearby. Neither's smiling, but something about their jaws says they're delighted to be here! Don't you wish you were? It's my idea, of course—the picture's simply another version of anywhere else. But aren't I everyone? There must be a way to see that sky, the bricks stacked at the end of our alley, while we stagger from one to the other, that's not so predictable, but larger, deeper than we imagined. That actually explains. Still, unless there's roast beef, pickles and relish, if not all the fixings, no one attends. This isn't a poem. There's nothing to hold.

WALK, WITH SALSA

(after "Crow on a Sunny Branch," color wood block print by Ohara Shoson, 1911-1915)

Hand's bleeding almost stopped, the broken
glass shattered in the sink is cleaned now.

The picture on the shelf above reminds me
there's always just one thing, two sides.

I should write back to the woman who sent it.
Aren't we finally old enough to not be

upset by such attention—your old boyfriends,
ex-husband, etc., ringing the doorbell,

while the women I loved fade with the flesh,
cells gone to memory? Touch me, here,

I used to think, not understanding
desire' s real point. I put salsa on everything

these days, trying to feel it, while my finger
is numb to her breast. Some theories claim

this disease is another virus, and maybe
the drug to cure it is on the way. Doctors

test my balance as I listen for the music
I always loved, stumble into the street.

THE STREET

Where's the file of good advice I've been
collecting for years, so I can reach in
each day for the one to lead me? Words
to say to the woman who opened

the cab door, and knocked me down
as I tried to slide by on my bike?
She kept saying how sorry she was
as I breathed on the asphalt, wondered

how long I'd have to lie there, what
had broken besides the new bike,
pain's general music keeping its dull beat
somewhere I couldn't find. Did I ruin

another pair of slacks? The white shirt?
There were other bodies standing over me,
there were cars, and trucks going by,
but I couldn't hear. The tracks overhead

were empty. Soon, I thought,
I'll pick myself up, walk into the office,
the meeting with the director about
next year's design. Two funerals,

my mother said she went to last week,
and I'd heard the names, though I didn't
know them. It's too hot again, the power
blinks off, and the day's work is gone.

Once I walked the six miles home
from downtown, so early I could count
everyone on my hands. And a week later,
I climbed to the top of a peak in Montana,

ate the last ripe peach I'd carried
from Colorado. Now the house I built
is home to bees and possums, windows
broken out, roof split and leaking. My legs

can't climb that ridge anymore. How long
till police come, an ambulance, the hospital?
Sweat dripped on the street as my eyes
waved. I didn't want to get up.

Continental Drift

But this ain't tuff nothin', as the country song goes. This is so much sun pouring over the crow's hoarse October there aren't any excuses. This is the body's nervous shake: too much room. Why don't you paint those steps? Leave sex out of it for once. I could have a cigarette, but I already tried that; one more thing to leave. It's the way the continental drift theories are blown apart by the facts—no signs of rupture at the supposed edges, and the micro-plate islands disconnected and drifting to run up against other coasts—where did they come from? The Appalachians long ridge buckled, folded, bent by what pressure? The Equator across Minnesota? There was comfort in that scale, watching myself shot backwards to the tiniest prick, then nothing, and yet, it might as well not be: throw in starvation, anarchy in Africa, and the personal trivia's apparent. The three-year old shot by a drive-by could be the jungle that once covered the interstate. A star's blink light years we try to measure. The steps need painting. I want her body rocking on me from above, my own racing on, the way it was. Another baseball season over? Despite the team's sad finish, they did better than we expected. We saw enough.

What She Knows

Something about money, while the flat tire
punctuates the vacation, and she

cuts off the conversation. Better this way?
Staring down the barrel I can smell

swamp oak aging, hear the tanager
through record cold. It's the same dream

I surely know better than to get
caught in. I can try a clever remark to get

her attention, explain the bleeding finger,
the grease spilling over the floor; so what

if it's not a permanent answer? He deserves
applause, they'll say. He knows expensive wine.

Otherwise it's the same view, over
and over, until her breasts descend

to sand and all the equipment's rusted.
The gray clouds look thick and tender.

I've never been so much in love.

Vacation

Traffic slows to a crawl as the music shakes the house. Vacuum the carpet now, sponge the table clean. After it's done, those brown white particles left on the table surface point like hands of another game: wild deuce? full house? Or some other language completely? They could mean anything; but then, a lifetime trying to pay attention thinks: bad news in a different disguise. All I have to do, the announcer reminds me, is make the call and wait. Disease stacked away, children finally old enough to ignore, the prize is on the way. Those kids having a ball, breaking the souvenirs we left downstairs while the wife's affair makes me love her even more. Now we know what's really important. There's wine, then sleep, death consigned to a leer from the outskirts. What a great vacation! I can't wait to see the pictures.

HAMLET, AGAIN

"'Tis bitter cold and I am sick at heart." (I,1,8)

But it's bright summer, air conditioner humming, new grass finally coming in, and the home team's reclining in the back, just where we expect them. Too bad for the fans, maybe, but look at that player's necklace, etc. The neighborhood flowers open. Still, we know something's wrong—the whole business of "equal" hangs on it. The body, for instance, fumbling out of control—maybe I can still get up the ladder, lop off a dead branch, but the empire's end is clear. There has to be a turn, a serious change, with history its fuel—personal story of rape and pillage, 1835. President denies allegations in breathtaking Caribbean. The war goes on in earnest . . .

Meantime, that famous twerp with the great words keeps coming. I spent the afternoon by the field, blue sky over bright celebration, and I could almost forget. Then the season's done and whatever has shown up won't repair the sagging porch. Maybe that's always the case, and the reason for those statues everywhere—a way to hold our attention in the wild country. They say Crazy Horse's nostril is the size of a house where he grows over the plains . . .

Mesquite Beans

The pod's curved and dry, faded cream with darker stains,
three tiny black dots, a small hole. Inside, there's a handful
of beans. And something else. At least there was. If

it's gone, what's left isn't safe to eat. Not that we won't.
You can barely breathe with that cold you've
caught, but next week you'll be screaming again.

It's almost your birthday, and new research reports
we can live decades longer than anyone knew.
Exercise every day, before long there's sure to be pills.

The cells that make sperm never stop. We might even
have sex again one day. These pods are long
past ripe and everything here is brittle.

Only a few bunches still hang from bushes,
scattered between cholla, saguaro, ocotillo.
Those cactus were so new to us, we couldn't

stay away, and my hand still hurts
from the one I caught yesterday—as if to shake me
to attention though the mind goes on to wander.

Under high tension wires along the highway,
scraps of metal, rubber, broken glass poke
and wallow amid brush, part of the landfill

the newspaper says will cost billions
to clean up with the rest of our debris.
Snow atop the Catalinas gone, a coyote howled

nearby, but though we waited, it didn't come back.
The whole country used to be this wild, and these are
the traces. The President's man resigned.

The "evil empire" is done. The alien wouldn't
stab the enemy his people wanted him to finish, but
we knew that in advance. We saw it on TV. He's half

human, a hero no matter how ugly. In the creek wash,
dirt, creosote bush, cloud of desert broom,
prickly pear, barrel cactus. At first bite

the beans taste paper, wood. Then sweet juice fills
the mouth, and all I want is more. They're delicious
to chew on a walk. But you can't eat them.

Screens

They were supposed to be fixed by today, now that we don't need them—though we will again. They'll keep the dust down, the bugs out; Though no screen will stop them all, I know; I'd describe them if I knew. How they slip in after the children are sleeping, sink into the nerves and send me after the gun. The brain's still clear: the taste is lousy, the barrel stiff, uncomfortable in the mouth. There must be other positions just as certain, where the feel's cleaner, the weapon simply a tool, apart from the mess of flesh. And I don't want any accidents. The angle's the least of the problem. Sorry, my son, my wife, really you're better off.

Last week someone brought you pills for the monthly pain, spermicide, a fuse. Was it burned out, or the replacement? So it's another story about sex, and what comes next. The Gods were going to teach us a lesson, while I was home, waiting. This time, the repairman finally came. He knew how to fix the machine, but though we both looked hard, we couldn't find the problem. The beautiful women get further away. The snow coming and going belongs to the neighborhood. There must be a way to avoid it, I think. Then I don't.

Body Art

With everyone shadow in the dark room, I didn't
see him at first. Sliding amid tables,
the shape was human, the body's curtain

shrunken to folds, skin stained blue, leather
codpiece the only garment. And small, a figure
suggesting not so much the animal we are,

but far from the garments we fit. The designs
on every inch hint ancient: blue, a patch
of red, a woman undressed over a thigh,

something else naked. But I don't want to know
the smell. I don't want to see
any eyes. It's not the pain this coat

announces that turns us away; rather, something
of the flesh itself, the small figure, a ghost
drifting amid conversations with their own

business where he doesn't belong. When he speaks,
we almost know the voice. The first design,
he was nineteen. He doesn't remember

which it was. Two more in the Navy, then this one,
and this. All his life he's lived
in this city, worked in the same factory.

Then it's quiet. Please eat these donuts,
the professor says. Someone is bringing
more juice. She shakes out long white hair.

A woman there to pierce flesh for jewelry
slumps in a chair against a wall. A young man
spreads out plastic gloves, vaseline,

turns on the engine to drive the needles
that etch the pictures. It's time
to leave. But we don't. We watch it buzz.

Monster As Leg

I've always known it was here. No dream at all, just the phone rings, and there's that smell, disgusting and irresistible. How like nothing I ever imagined: no face at all, nothing the body registers—But what's this leg shaking, this weight the chest hauls? Maybe it's only mind; but there's the flesh, whether or not I see it. A shock in some ways, until I realize it's always been here, just not in this shape. I remember spring on that roof in the woods, the sound of Canada geese coming back to the marshes, scarlet tanagers floating in the trees.. Once, I climbed the ladder, hauled up the chain saw, cut the dead limbs. Pathetic, what it's come to?

Listen, I actually walked a few steps today. It isn't "making the best" of anything. It's making. No one said it was easy. The footings for this porch were bad concrete from the start, though I had no way of knowing then, and the railing was never fit right. But the deck will hold us; and if I'm careful, I can lean on the rail.

Prayer, With Kings

The kings are coming around the corner,
heavy steps, and the whole street
shivers in rain. The radio explains
the market, the championship season.

The beggars trail their torn
coats. Then the magician, the fool,
guns, flowers. Open the door!
It's seventy degrees in Pittsburgh!

The queen's home for lunch, and to walk
her dog. She has to tell everyone
the good news. The tattooed lady
ignites the cannon, the cat in the shoe

blows smoke rings. The Duke of Shovels
uncovers a breast, a lock of hair,
white in the river. There goes
the secret. Now it's snowing

all over the castle. The radio
stopped. But the ark isn't finished.
The captain bows his head, leans
on a scrap of rail. Tell me

mistah bone, now the skin's failed
with the nerves, does the food really come?

TRAPDOOR

At first the old witch could be grandma grinning
at the boys she caught snooping. She's got two
of her own, grown evil louts, and a look stops
one from hurting the kids. The voice seems kind.
Then the eyes narrow. The kids found the car in the garage
sprayed with bullets, but the louts found them.
The trouble's getting serious. There's something
in the basement, chained to a chair, spitting
animal grunts, a plate of food just out of
reach. One lout taunts it. You still haven't
got a job. See the mess your children are making?
Any of those guys you could've had make more
than I ever will. Unemployment figures worst in a decade.
Eight-year old shoots another in class.
And that's a good neighborhood. My own grandma
left the scolding to grandpa. When we broke
the basement window we caught the train home before
he found out. That house was bright
to the bottom, old coal bin rebuilt for storage, walls
of napkins, coffee, soup against the next disaster.
Grandpa shined our shoes on the caddy he built there,
each drawer's hardware labeled exactly. Took us
shopping for toys, gave us quarters, jokes, rides
each night to end at the Dairy Queen. We loved to visit.
The rules were clear. We couldn't play in the basement.
We carried down clothes, detergent, when Grandma
did laundry and told us how she used to scrub on the corrugated
washboard that still leaned in the corner, squeeze
everything to sheets through the old ringer. Now, gray water
shot from a black hose, boiled in the concrete tubs,
and drained as the machine rumbled. She told us this

was easy. When we finally see
the thing chained and grunting, one eye an inch
higher than the other, huge pointed saucers for ears,
we laugh. It's awful. It's human
and ruined. We can't quit staring. In the basement room
in the movie, the hero kid hears company coming,
crawls under a fireplace grate. There's something
in the dust. He blows. It's a handle. He opens the door.
The bad guys are coming fast. He calls his friends,
and they all climb in, pull the door shut behind.
They're going down.

*

When I get to the hospital, you're dressed, sitting up
and reading. The operation's put off a week for a cold
that would make the anesthesia trouble. For a while
we'll pretend the whole thing won't be. Let's have lunch,
and you'll drive back to the vacation you've planned all year.
It's an estate, there's a porch off your room, acres of prairie, field,
old woods, trimmed paths, gardens of iris and daisy.
There's a bike you can ride to the cafe in town, books lining
the shelves, and quiet. And time. If the food's not
quite what you'd choose, someone else is making it, someone else
is cleaning up. Thursday, we'll come to visit. But tonight
I promised our children another movie they want.
A doll's infested with murder. He grips a knife, staggers
toward a mother, her son, everything we love. Our own
are frozen as deer in headlights. Then one turns away,
buries his eyes in the couch. The other says he's "not scared"
over and over, eyes dark pools spread to their limit.
An animal faces the terrible god, dropping

forever in black. Nobody wants this. It's June,
sweet peas and columbine, tomorrow a barbecue. Barely
old enough for school, our kids haven't met
the one on the bus who'll rip up the pictures
they made for Mom, who'll punch one in the eye,
demand a dollar or else. Of course they're on the way.
And a home run, a campfire in the mountains, the long
conversation of friends. A woman. But the doll
is bleeding, his arm's shot off, then his head, and
he's still coming. Next week, the long needle
goes in, scrape and probe delivering news. Gap
between rich and poor grows. Another bank fails.
Recluse who lived in garden found dead.

*

And then she couldn't remember. Not all at once, but the slips
widened, neurons misfiring, as if a synapse
opened, then another, a flock, and the map's one
lost tangle, vital directions crayoned over
by the baby who found it to play with.
"Would you like a piece of fruit?"
That baby doesn't mean anything, after his own treasure:
how does it taste? And the route's not some
idle conversation—whether to go or not,
which way, how, then the whole idea simply
abandoned with another "oh, well . . ." We're too far already,
there's no going back. There's no trail. Dust
her tables never had thickened. The kitchen counter
stayed empty. After a meal at the restaurant, she wondered
when we were going to eat. Then she didn't.
"Would you like a piece of fruit?" The cracks

in the ceiling plaster spread and yellowed,
grandpa's tools hung in place as he dozed amid
the talk. Then a dozen of us stood on plywood
laid over red mud, each taking a turn to dump
three shovels into the pit. A strand of my sister's hair
blew against snow, and I blinked to notice
its graywhite color. When my wife stepped toward the shovel,
she was turned away—ancient law forbidding
the pregnant woman such commerce with death.
A thousand dollars, grandpa said the coffin cost,
each one harder for him to let go these days,
though he had more than he'd ever imagined.
It was the one fact we could say after the smooth pulleys
sunk her to the bottom. He pulled the slivers
from my palm so gently I hardly felt it, as we sat on the couch
watching TV that night years before.
And on Saturday mornings he took us to the office,
let us play with the machines. When we got back,
she always had lunch ready. Then it was him.
Filled with my clothes, his old dresser shipped
from their bedroom smelled like it for weeks.
Would you like a piece of fruit?

*

I was amazed how silent the schoolroom fell when I first
tried the story. I told them to look under the bed
and imagine. There's the trapdoor. There's the handle.
It isn't a dream. No one has to go,
but they're brave. I told them the trip can be long, to bring
what they thought they might use. They chose
a jacket in case of cold, knife, rope, kleenex & cookies;

a penny, a mirror for magic. They stared
at the stone, iron rings, rusted chains, the tight passage
I described. They wanted to know
where it led. I gave them sun through a window,
grass, any animals they could invent for this planet inside.
They gave me TV monsters, guns, a "unacone."
The windows of the old building were permanently
sealed, light dim, numbers painted on the door long faded.
Static and orders broke into the story.
"Mrs. Givens, see Mr. Williams. Shana Deshay
to the office. Use the south exit after lunch . . . "
So Mari pokes Jesse and he hits back to bruise.
So Ronald takes out a cigarette, points it
at the teacher. The girl who can't learn keeps running
into her father's sex, flounces out of the room.
Who can follow the plot? How do you spell
"explosion"? They all want to laugh. Then the teacher
walks out, someone giggles, someone screams
an inch from a gun in a pocket. They're insects crawling
over the trashcan's side, wriggling for light
they don't know. At lunch, din rattles the ceiling,
food gone in a minute. The door's unchained. For a few
minutes they're out. But their stories always
end with death, a dream to wake from, no magic.
The treasure's further down those steps.

*

Red carnations on this table are lovely,
and when you come back, we'll ride our bikes
to the play downtown. I need the exercise, we'll feel better
even if the play's lousy. Maybe we'll have sex again

if we can find time. Elections are coming, and
the new candidate looks sure to win; he promises
money for doctors, good schools, "real change."
Not that we think he can help our salary,
but we're going to vote. The woman with the hearing aid
next to you in the theatre didn't mind the fireworks, thought
the dialogue tedious, and we agree. We all loved
the train tracks, colored lights, arrangements of bodies.
If the movement was slow, solitude & slavery & no place
to go—ideas half a century stale—in the New Order,
there's no other power. We need someone to understand.
Be tough on Japan. Bring jobs home. Keep the bombs ready.
Stop those drugs. Fritzy Carlson swung the neighbor's cat
by the tail, let it fly to vomit and disappear in brush
behind the garage. Dickie Olson gave me a cup of
"root beer." I brought it to my lips before he told me
it was his piss. It's not just in those projects.
Your friend's story was true: when the rich boy's Dad
broke his neck, the prince the boy dreamed lost the kingdom.

*

At the bottom of the stairs in that movie, the sky's
a gray ceiling, air dim but clear. It's a huge room,
and no way out but the way they've come.
And there's the ship—ancient, perched
in some dry dock, sails long gone, another century's rigging
intricate and dumb. The pirates are bones. There's gold,
piles of it, though they have to leave a share for the skeleton
captain, patch still over what was an eye. Now the problem
is getting back. And here come the bad guys.
But the fat kid they made fun of made friends

with the freak. It's a boy stronger than any, and the weapons
the crooks try won't work. Those punks are sacks
he tosses back. The kids get home, rich. And the doll
in the other film? Burned to ash, a spirit
dwindled to smoke at the credits. This morning, a child
came to my bed, real and warm. Of course he wanted you.
But dozed then, and woke happy to me, and ran
downstairs bright through the rest of the day.
He doesn't know why you're not here. He plays on.
Tomorrow you'll come, go back to the hospital,
and we'll wait. The kids want to see that movie again.

The Kingdom

Gold and whores a thousand years announced that
heaven: another feast, wine, music. So the Pope
slept with the daughter, who slept with her brothers.
So the king beheaded another wife. Let's torture
the infidel, march to the next border.

But that was another century. Everyone says
this Cardinal's "a regular guy." His house has more rooms
than we can guess, old, square chimneys on top,
a Mercedes in the drive. It's the only yard
at the end of the block. Blood and gold

leaves stir the sky, the park across the street,
the museum of history on the corner. There's no sound
inside the house, then muffled chimes, and the back door
opens. Plain as her white habit, the nun takes
my letter: his message reaches us all: I'm a Jew,

I want to tell his story. They say he'll write back
thanks, but there's no time to talk, nothing
new to say. The child walking to school
is shot in the back, a car wraps the bridge's frame,
the father is gone. Face twisted with the loss, the throat

shuts, but we can't look away. Every day there's more
pain. Don't we love this death, the wild blue water,
the trees' fire? Hold this hand. We're alive.
So the Indians watched the geese circle these banks
as the buffalo swept the prairie, huddled

for the invaders' guns, dove off cliffs. So the priest
drinks with the mayor as they toast the re-election.
Steel and glass blink in the sun, and it's Halloween, winter,
spring again. But the basement of this house has a hole
I've got to fix, an upstairs window that needs a new frame.

The Cardinal leads another prayer. Everyone knows
he's dying, and we can't resist the details:
he's thanking the priests, blessing the schools,
writing to the Supreme Court. He's trying to breathe.
The river that emptied into the lake flows the other way.

His letter never comes. Now, he says, he's free.

Fasting

For some forgiveness: of this body, these cells, lurching into the wall. Still breathing, I say, if anyone asks. I can't smell the perfume anymore, but I remember the voice, the skin's texture. Billions vanish while the sun floods the floor. The planet was right over there. Old friends were so happy to see us—Sharon, for instance, or whatever her name was—her long black hair, musical laugh . . . Of course I shouldn't be thinking about her, what with the garden I have to make my son weed, the carpenter I've got to nag to fix the work he didn't get right. But then I've got it wrong again. Where did I leave the new blade for the saw? The nails? All the tools are on the shelves downstairs, and the hardware store's open. It even sells food for the cat the children love. Forgive me for these mistakes. The animal has to be fed.

Holy Day

And things were going so well—you winning the drawing, me getting the raise as our team soared to the lead, the screaming almost gone. Ok, so I hit the kid again. He deserved it. Pain, tears, ice to the spot, but no bruise anyone could see. He's got to learn. Besides, he's fine now; I'm the one sick with it. Isn't this sadness enough? It could be an echo of the famous trial, wife beaten and murdered with her boy friend, the killer set free. He's so sorry. We think it helped him to be famous. But the rest of us? The doctor injects the serum, we get tired, immunity breaks down, we're overcome. Cancel my subscription, turn off that popular song. Say it: AvenuMalkenu: for the sin that I have sinned against thee. A day fasting, hope for another year, and better; now do you understand? Luckily, we've stopped expecting that.

II. SPRING TRAINING

Dance

1
There's something new no word can name.
We've seen the pictures, gray mush
the cells ooze; another way of saying: us.
Men and women in gray jackets squint through
microscopes, convene in a room
we don't see. Music, food, bright sun
outside are part too; though we're guessing.
We're breathing. I can watch clouds
gather, dissolve out the window,
the football game on the TV mounted
against the wall at the end of the bed
you lie in, with the same blank
that joins me to the rest. I sip
whatever this is, stare at the end of
the tunnel, the clouds that mass and
roil. Something gets in the way.
I'm trying to watch the ball.

2
How much I've wanted to be brilliant,
that old stupidity rising from what?
Ambition, traffic, slate skies over
all the beautiful women? I'm calling again,
as the walls close in, and I slump exhausted,
barely breathing. But such melodrama's only
a piece of the boredom, which is another
word for terror. The flesh is crazy
to be noticed—frantically rubbing,
brushing, dressing itself for the affair.
Then I step back to see something else
replace it—the tube for the medicine, the place

to insert the needle, exact details of
a process I've been moving toward a lifetime
without knowing. I'm late again, but
I'm coming—by train, by bus, by foot, and
she's waiting with the prescription., smiling
and deadly, surrounded by our children.
It's a fate more delicious than food,
than the sexual scent pinning me in
its oily churn. Still alive, in other words.
What wonderful clothes! What sleep!

3
Water seeps between lungs and
chest. The surgeon's mechanical smile's a buzzer
I hear when he says the answer is simple:
seal the lungs to the chest wall;
the pain's slight, and nothing goes wrong.
My stomach's acid. Cops come to the room
and tell us we have to quiet down. We can't
drink the whiskey we've brought.
In the other room where they take us,
I ask the woman in charge if she thinks
we're not hurting enough. The TV says
guerillas across the world have blown up
buildings. Thousands are dead.

4
You laid in bed with your friend, watched
Captain Hook on TV, and we loved
the quiet stare. They'll get rid of the cells
gone wrong. And then? There's the party

you missed, the one you will, the soccer game,
skateboard, ice cream. Everything in the room
shines, though the scent of the dump
we passed on the way this morning
rises again, as if to remind me: we're on
the same plank, pushed to the end
we can't see. There must be a way off.

5
Instructions, weather, language
shunted nowhere don't explain
the machine that stands up squawking,
drives a blank stall into mind with
the usual background hum.
It's breathing, isn't it?
                    But I want
to forget. Call it doubt, extinction,
nothing that has words. I can only
stare at the sign fixed to the truck
outside: "Information on paying
your property taxes here."

6
Squinting through the crack in the door,
you can almost miss the tube hooked
in the body's opening, delivering
the drug. There's no Superman cape,
no hair on fire. They call it medicine.
Another rerun flickers on TV, his scalp shines
between wispy hairs, arms shrunken
beneath the blanket. Alive, we tell whoever

asks how we are—a joke we invite
with the discomfort. As if pain is a flag
we can wave against the dirt we're
bolting into, while an army gathers
to answer the call. From certain angles
it seems to work; we savor plums
a friend we haven't seen for years
surprised us with. I never liked her much,
but now? The fruit gleams, the taste
bitter, but the juice keeps dripping.

7

The scale says he's not
getting smaller, though he's sure
he must be. His hair's falling
away, and the ball in my stomach
shallows my breath, stalls me
in place, though it weighs nothing.
I remember standing a year ago
against the blank kitchen wall
for the contractor's photo.
They'd emptied the room completely
to start the new one, and the cabinets
they installed hold more than we need.
The white stove gleams, though
the halogen light's never been
bright enough. Dropped too often,
the switch doesn't work anymore.
But the light's never burned out.
The orchid we put on the new table's
blooming. The winter snow is

gone. I should say something
tender then, and I want to. But no
sound can explain his skin, a touch
more than flesh can recall; where
we're all heading; that no saying
can change. I'll order another switch.

8

In the hospital hall I'll never
forget, we waited for the elevator
to take us out. I can see the gray doors,
posters for prayer meetings, and I can
hear me repeating the lines you taught me
until you grinned I had it:
    "If your friends can't dance, if they really
    can't dance, they ain't no friends of mine."
The clothes are gone now, which is what
you'd want; and would be the first
to tell me to forget the museum
we can't stop making of what was left.
The ragged scraps don't fit anyone,
even as you become them, as the brother
you left, who you never wanted,
any more than he wanted you, becomes
you. But can't I save anything?
Each day, my own disease shortens
any walk, makes it harder to watch
the rest who can. Whatever spirit
you might be nods at the passing,
sure as I know, each day, I must.

Spring Training

1
A thousand miles away, the players are
practicing again. Sun floods the building
across the alley that's being redone so
richer tenants can see the field when
the new season begins. Beneath the seats,
the old green scoreboard, they're grooming
the field. The stadium will be ready. We can't
see it, but we know the signs—trucks, dirt,
piles of sod on the sidewalks. You never
really cared about the game, but noticed that
I seemed to; and sometimes you asked
about it, as if to please me. I can feel
your hands holding my face; hear your voice
in patches, drumbeats, notes of other
music, sounds coming further apart.

2
And so, you drift; or I do, as
we all do. Nothing sad about that.
Your mother's patching cracks in walls,
sanding a chair. A glass of wine sits
on a table. An antique car shines
through the window, and gray snow
piles in the alley have almost gone.
More metaphor? These days I'm grateful
for anything I understand: the finger
plugged in an ancient dike, a joke,
an arm's brush; no matter it's always

too little. They've knocked the corner
off the building next door and put in
new windows for a wider view of the field
they face. Next week another season begins,
and all over the city, fans are getting excited.
This time, they really believe the team
will win. Everyone hopes it's true.

3

It's the first day of your school's vacation,
bright and cold, and three friends
of yours were here with your brother.
Each of their mothers called, looking
for them, sons slipping further away,
which we all expect, though no one's
ever ready. You'd be at least as gone.
I don't remember if they'd started
working on that building when you were
here, or if you ever saw it. I only
remember the couch where I laid
with you the last time, my arms
around your belly, blue veins webbed
across it, your arms and legs thinned
to sticks. And your voice. Not the odd
high-pitched almost squeak of that
last day, but the one yelling snotty
and sure, telling me exactly what
you were going to do, no matter
what I said. The one that whispered,
"I love you so much, Dad. Good night."

4

We only want a day moving chairs
from one room to another, buying soap
and pills at the drugstore, vegetables
for dinner. This isn't forgetting.
I ate apples and cheese for lunch.
Your brother did his homework.

And you, left to idea while someone
throws a football across the street
to someone? I'm talking to
your picture again, the one from
last summer, where you're grinning,
legs crossed, heady and sure as
you'd learned to be. It's quiet
a minute, then your brother breaks in,
wearing my sweater, and calls me
a name we laugh at, as you would,
and loudly, and more. He's you too,
as he has always been, though both of you
hated the thought. "Have you forgiven me
yet?" he yells at his mother. She's mad
he didn't do all the chores he was told to.
"I took out the trash," he yells; and I can
look through the window, clear
again now, into the dark. And I will.

5

Your mother's on the way to
Florida, tennis, and the story beginning

"then" is mine alone, with the blank
that follows. In the woods I left to
be here twenty-five years before,
stunted jackpines scattered among
breathtaking whites sway in the sky.
Wild rice grows to October, deer and
berries in summer. I love to visit
and will again, as our old friend
does here. Would it matter if
you came up too? A crane boom hangs
at the corner of the building they're remaking
across the alley. Traffic's parked solid
down the street. I can hear your laughter,
or the idea of it I imagine.
It's Sunday, I notice, which must
mean something. The music keeps playing

6

(after "Visiting Tsan, Abbot of Ta-Yun" by Tu Fu)

Apple blossoms open again, glowing
white on blue. My stiffened fingers
stop at work once
thoughtless as breath. I walk in the sun,
halfway around the block, stumble
into a fence. The jacket's torn.

Annabel

The kitten whose mother you loved purrs
and settles on my hand. She was born and
named in the house that kept her
while we watched the Mediterranean,
drank wine, and drove through the history
spread on the other side of the ocean:
a castle Phoenicians built; a village
behind walls; the mountains
that held back armies. They're all
you left us, and nothing
we could imagine; as the ancient curse
about getting one's wish expands into

the one life I've become. Today,
the friend who lay with you once in
the hospital bed left a flower
at your grave, reminding me of all
we are as the city waits under snow
you never saw. All night it fell.
Once I would have shoveled it, or set
you and your brother to the job.
Still, it's beautiful, and white
against the ball of fur humming
on the sill. And there's other work.
Already it's started to melt.

Keren Ami*

First light, I woke to your mother
crying without a sound beside me.
She was thinking of you, she said,
and she didn't want to stop. Last night
she wrote a letter quitting the congregation
we'd joined so you could learn the religion
we came from. Sundays I drove you
there and waited by the lake behind,
or in its library, while you practiced
the ancient language I'd long stopped
believing could matter. I still hope I'm wrong.

That temple served us through your end,
though whatever ancient promise
the words brought has gone with you.
She wants to send the charity cash
you saved to give those poorer
back to the temple that gave you
the can to decorate and take home.
You hoped the money would help
someone who needed more; and that might
help you. The season's first cold has settled in.
Leaves turn gold and rust. Across the world,
an army blows up buildings. The war
goes on. They say it never ends.

*Hebrew: gift to my people

STORY

I'm trying to believe I'm not talking
just to myself—a mark, I know, of crazy.
Like the long walks in strange towns
I took years before, the late night calls
to voices I thought I knew. But who
were they? It was always too late,
and "she" was never there; although
the wandering didn't mean I was lost.
At least, I didn't think so. I always found
the way back to the place where I slept.

I've been here for years, and I know
sleep is only delay against the rest
we can't help chasing, Still, I'm grateful
for the story, the company joined
to hear it, and laugh, the roar of
the crowd leaking through the windows.

The Catacombs

The carved lion is under repair;
only the slab where it stood
remains in the street. The human bones
lie underneath, the line to see them

curled around the corner in the rain.
Most come from our country, speaking
that language where death is barely
admitted, though many here know

Baudelaire is buried nearby, and Rimbaud,
and Jim Morrisson. You loved his music;
it keeps coming back; and here you are again.
We were going to bring you with us,

and the brother you left, who's
become you, sure as I hear him yell,
"No way!" Loud as you would.
But no sound is foreign enough

to disguise the voice that could be
yours, the sounds nowhere we go
can stop. If only I had a scooter, I hear
it say, a new machine, legs faster

than engines. It's your voice, in a language
so familiar we think we know it, though
we don't understand. The city has
never heard of you or your absence.

The stench that once came from
the bones is another story I'm left in
this cafe to imagine, as your brother
walks underground with your friend, staring

at skulls. They're shouting, thinking of jokes,
stories they'll tell when they come back.
They've already passed me. They're climbing
up stones, heading toward the day.

Circus

(after Kenneth Koch)

I remember reading "The Circus," the one
about the first the poet wrote with
that name, that he thought was better.
This one remembered his time in Paris,

friends he loved, a life everyone likes
to imagine, and never existed, and everyone
must leave. Some friends had died by the time
he wrote the new one, but nostalgia wasn't

the point, though the longing was there,
and sadness, and I remember looking
down at the ragged couch where I was reading,
next to the fake fireplace, the aquarium with

the bright fish I used to stare at while headphones
blasted rock n' roll nights I couldn't sleep;
and I cried. I was young. I don't know why.
I never wanted to go to Paris. Sun poured

through the kitchen where I made the bread
we ate, and over the porch in back where
I took the poem to read again. The next year
we left the city for somewhere else.

We didn't know where it would be, which was
the point, and that it could only happen
once, though we didn't know what
that would mean either. In the woods far north

we stopped and cleared some land, and built
a house with our own hands, heated with oak
I cut and hauled. I loved the place, but I couldn't
find enough work to pay, and I left it too. I was lost.

They were all good days, which is what memory
makes of most history for those lucky enough
to read it and not think too far past
the details. What I wanted was the very thing

I'm doing now each day. The woman
I married after that one left. The children
I couldn't imagine. I know it's luck,
and I miss it all at times, as most do,

and some of it more, and always.
The son whose death I keep trying
to understand, for instance, which seems
another subject completely; but then,

it isn't. Two years after his end, we've gone
to Paris, felt it gorgeous and rich as
the stories. Some days the sky's so clear
it shines. Or doesn't. His brother comes home.

III. NATURE

House Work

So here you are again. Or is it me, with
stump fingers, the cross-threaded screw stopping
me short? Like the house in the woods my wife
those days drove us to keep building, though I
couldn't get the parts to fit any way I imagined?
I swore the work could never be worth it,
and now, every nail is magic I love to
recount, as if I'd always believed the religion.
A lesson in hauling what's bound to be left?

Then the child died, and all the rest
is words. Weather. Choose a name.
Think of a familiar face, breathing you don't
notice until it all goes South. Or
North. There's always another view—
spaghetti with mustard, say; a white sock
stuck in an elevator. We're used to
the complaining; after the bills, the trash
has to get emptied. I only want the geese,
brandy, the swamp down the road from that
house we built and lived in. Then she's here,
like you, another time, somewhere else.
Does it fit together then?
                                        Seen from another
angle, the answer is "E: all of the above,"
and it doesn't take genius to get it. But the facts
don't tell us how to use them, and we're
back to plotting a way down the steps,
to a night of faces we know. When I fall,
I have to think someone will help me up,
nothing broken. There's laughter. There's music.

Horses

Music and wine, and the blue, blue lake spreading into the sky—simply nothing to hate. Sure the body can barely make it up the stairs anymore, but isn't that another blessing waiting for me to understand? Like the vanished sex, leaving the children in its wake, more beautiful than I could imagine. Did I really think that house we built in the woods would last? It's just that the clearing left when it vanished swallowed the hardware so completely. I had to buy a new drill and now I can't find the chuck key. I've even got the case the old one came in, all the bits in order, spotless in the original drawer. Plenty of people understand the difficulties, but that doesn't drive a nail. "Structure over aesthetics" the dead author said, as he slapped up the rack to hold the saddles, dented the wall on the way. Those horses are long gone.

Saved

Like that dream where she really wanted you—gleam of skin, breast, cock—the usual compensations? Then trash on waking, mixed with the swollen leg, throbbing while someone tore up the back door in the night, and the house was stripped. All over the world the shooting goes on. Then the doorbell rings and the pain is actually gone. With the notes buried in the counter's daily junk pile, you had no idea you'd even entered. Now it's another city. No paradise, but all the blood, sex, he, she, flushed away. It's not all luck. You have to pay attention, send in the entry. Now, I can quit this stupid job, take over the building, gifts to all our friends. We can be lost again, actual ghosts wandering the streets. All we've got to do is keep out of sight. Of course that's impossible. It's time to clean the gun.

Raining Poem

"In Lima, it is raining. In Lima, it is raining."—César Vallejo

And so on, with streets, walls, figures composing
the mood setting's designed to reveal.
Careful arrangement's essential for us to believe

the events that collect the meaning: this
old guitar blues, new with organ; the aged waitress
setting down coffee; a handful of voices at

different tables. But the pit in the stomach,
the clenched fist no one sees is driving. Caissons
crack, split, crumbled stone and dust fill the space.

Is that why Vallejo repeats the line?
As if to absorb the dust? It worked for him,
an idea clear as music falling from

this ceiling, that I'd so much rather
attend than the details I can't seem to
arrange and keep returning: the white

beard of her lover; his mouth and
hands on her skin, wiping away
the room she was happy to leave.

It's sunny here, but cold, which means
nothing beside the light pole I've wandered
outside to lean against as the scenes

continue. Should I add the "Indigo!" sign
from the strip mall across the street?
Sudden and striking, maybe it could

help explain how she forgot what
the husband's learning would mean.
Or the woman who just came in and

sat at the empty table behind me—
I can make her whatever I want.
Now, the wind picks up. It blows harder.

Morning With Lilac,

bacon, sun, and you were the scent—good news we knew would end; but this time, maybe not, at least for a long time. The open newspaper adds the burned wreck of a face, and even that's ok, as if the shock makes us "good citizens," part of the machine we've learned to operate. Not exactly comfortable, shifting around this confinement, but we know what to do. Let's not talk about pain, I'm just never hungry this early. When the great idea dissolves again, I'll clean up the mouseshit, have a glass of that good red wine. The burning isn't ours, and the faint wish that it was is another symptom. The idea? Remember the birds—gulls I think, though they could have been parrots—brilliant colors emptied into the fog, so they were shadows carved on the pilings at the end of the breakwater. The feel of mist. Cold, and sharp. And further away, a frayed ribbon trailing after something squat and distant, a factory, like an old schoolbook photo we didn't give the right attention. I was only trying to get home and the tire went flat. Dear ----, are you coming soon? Do I know you at all?

THE CUP

"When anomalous information reaches a certain threshold, it's job is to force the left hemisphere to revise the entire model and start from scratch." —*New York Times*

It's those new galaxies, something we can't see that the experts know must be there. How else explain being here at all in the face of this flying apart? Winter rain, sneeze and cough, another friend's divorce—nothing new—but the award's there too; and that great sex the porn movie imagines. So the picture's changing again. Lucky for the pills, filing off the edges. Tonight I'll be able to sleep, get to the job in the morning and stand it. I can even admire the new door the carpenters hung—a little off square, but the thing closes.

It's all involved with the dark matter—the WIMP theory vs. another I've already forgotten. Either there are billions of stars we can't see, burned out, whose gravity holds the rest together, or—? I know the information is vital, though no one really understands it. One day you're lifting, turning, everything in the ordinary way, then the arm stops working. The phone rings, and nobody's there. It's spring, complete with dirty snow, and by the time all the data's collected, summer. You're parched, the cup sits on the table, brimming with pure cold water. If only you could drink.

THE FUN BEGINS

anywhere—laughter, a little fear, a dash of sex—the usual weather, with just a pinch of surprise. It's all in the way they're mixed. Two teaspoons flour, a dash of sugar, water, salt, and it's rising. Yes, I'm bored as you are with the whole process. Let's try some bright paper, a balloon doily, say. Meatloaf, grapefruit, plastic or glass? This is the situation, and no one knows a cure The debate is endless. She's so pretty, and I'm in love with the voice, even the screaming. Just another drama queen? Nothing to do with bad blood, only the usual cells' silent grinding—fall, winter, etc. rotating outside the window. It always starts when you're not looking, then it grabs you, keeps you awake through all the music and keeps on going. When it's over, if it ever can be, here she is, and you can't get away—a combination you never could have expected. What more does anyone want?

"One stops being a child only when one realizes that telling one's troubles doesn't necessarily make it any better." The rest is up to you.

After Sweet Jane

(for DCH)

You've never written, but you're always
there, when I can unstring

the story, rock n' roll animal, gone
back to the old religion. I'm still

on that roof where we first watched the night
turn in our smoke. Call it Jesus-- a ship

floating over our heads that none of us quite
sees-- what keeps you driving those nails.

Then you must know, and hear the one sound
in the dark. So this is metaphor?

Maybe. And maybe half they say of the Name
is true. Understand, I want it

all to be. I want the skin so clear
we can love it purely; this disease

I never imagined to vanish. Each death
edges closer, as the mind

bobs into the door; and I only know
this Midwest day, summer again, too early,

too hot, and green as the one
you left. Surely someone is listening.

That music was the very planet, resolving
the distance, and we were there,

naked in the mountains, the desert, and surely
on the way. Now tell me what happened.

More Fun

No one believes in this war. The wounded? They're playing football, planning a trip to the ocean, whiskey and conversation with old friends. The newspapers announce the latest agreement, the new mayor who swears to honor the hero. The cold wind cleans out the drunks, and the broken glass littering the alley is part of the celebration. Sure there's death, but it's not ours. The captured pilot deserves what he gets for flying that border. The woman raped and dismembered in her hut? I hope she recovers. Her children's blank cries are the words left over, falling about the quiet rooms on our green boulevard. We could change the station, but it helps us remember why we're here: this expanse of lawn, close to shopping and the new foreign restaurant, the food so strange and interesting. We knew who to vote for, and it must make a difference even if we can't see. We got new furniture. If we're a little short when the bills come, it proves we finally belong. Surely they'll punish the scum who did it. Send pictures of the fun. I like to remember.

NATURE

Then it's spring. Or is it snow sparkling the pines? Either way, the moon's a copper coin, says nothing, and we quiver in its music. Time for silence. How the stars hold us. How this, O that, O endless . . The group attending is small, but bigger all the time, a chorus, swelling wherever you listen. Remember all the darkness? One bone? Magic, we cry, magic, and here's the music in the dream. Everyone's trying to eat the right thing. But don't forget the skin part—the way she's taking off her clothes, and he is. We're paying attention, we're upstairs praying. When the war's finally over, we feel deliciously free, though the new refugees do smell a little funny. We welcome them gladly, at least from a distance, but how to explain the carefully ragged dress, all the accidents cultivating the "casual look"? Imagine talking to an old friend, making it clear: I'm glad to see you've put on a few pounds, you look much more solid. The new wife's much prettier, though she is strung tight; sometimes it seems she'll never stop talking. Meantime, someone's pried off the back door, swept out all the expensive gadgets and we didn't hear a thing. The explosions are closer, more frequent. They're the same voices, just pitched to a new timbre. Then we understand: we have gone back to nature.

Our Religion

We all leave something: the story about the ants, ducks, and bees, say. Horses of pure stone in the stable outside the castle. But how did it happen? Ancient magic, holy warriors from Rome, Africa, the East. We've got to be saved. The chants still the excitement as the sun pours and pours, lighting the snow that decorates the city, and we're on the way to church, it's a real holiday. We're religious, our guns are holy. The war goes on in that ancient country, and we're praying for the boys we've sent to join. Surely peace is at hand.

In the castle there's a door with three locks. One for each of the brothers? Way too simple. The center of the door is glass, we can see the old man waiting at the table on the other side. He's always been there. The third time we call he gets up, unlocks the door and invites us in. He feeds us, gives us wine, puts us to sleep in his own room.

In the morning, of course, there are tasks: The princess lost a thousand pearls, and the smart ones can't find them. They're turned to stone. But the animals the simple brother saved are glad to help. The ants find the pearls, the ducks bring up the key to the princess's chamber, and the bees know the youngest daughter by the honey on her sleeping lips.

Notice how quickly we slid over the sex? It's always there, in the center, and she is gorgeous, but we're not going to be distracted. Our child's been working two days, his desk is almost clear, books and models in perfect order. When the castle is freed and the other brothers return to their lives, the simple one who saved them marries the beautiful girl. Everyone joins the celebration. We know the peace won't last, but maybe it'll hold for a while, and we can keep making the payments, afford another car when this one stops for good.

The Old Ball Game

(In memory of Harry, Jack)

Here's the night grandpa took my hand, teased out
the slivers I'd caught from the wooden walk
I jumped on behind his house. The crack

in the garage door where I couldn't stop throwing
the ball. The bare toilet, and the guy blowing
the joint he snuck in the cell where the cops

hauled us for scalping tickets. Waiting
for bail, I was still hoping to make the last few innings.
Our kid broke another window. Another hero

is dead. Over the plaques of the long gone stars
Harry raved about, handfuls called by his voice
stand mute in front of torn newspaper pages,

a hand written "So long," beer bottles, a pile
of flowers. We love that old song, the long summers
he delivered all the oblivion any voice could.

Of course it's raining again. A shopping mall
edges toward the stadium. The war
comes closer each day I wake up; sure as the day

I won't. I'm listening. And I will.

Chicken

I've always liked it—barbecued, with wine, mushrooms, pineapple, plain, anything—No bones to catch in the throat, it's almost sweet, like—Well, how do you describe a taste? The couch where we sat to eat it was worn and soft, the light dim. There were carrots and rice on the side, sherry to finish. I was hungry and the food was hot. Then why was I so desperate to leave?

I've explained the dream over and over– It's not the disease bending me over, the one that took my son. Left by itself, our porch tilts toward collapse while the flesh dissipates and Sharon lies quiet as sleep, awaiting the attention she's sure she's always deserved.

Each bite then is another step, more—the only real progress, if I can see from the right angle. I could backtrack, but the essential supplies are already gone, and so is the trail. Outside, a car alarm wails through the night, keeping the neighborhood up, as if to remind me of the danger; and I remember when the noise brought my son to this bed. It was the skin's sweet chance to feel surprised alive, breathing in black. Sure we're all dying. Then have another piece. There's still some left.

Music Lesson

All this time and I haven't
understood; motes slipping mysteriously
past, as if some kind of spirit,
while the pigeons clump and
waddle on the corner of the lot.

A dismal season, some would say,
and now that it's over, only
the unswept scraps the crowd dropped
on their way out remain as evidence.
But the music still echoes

if I'm quiet enough, those bright
and shimmery days returning
in quick snapshots. It's Bach
filling the basement, notes
bruised and difficult as the hands

of the child driven to make them.
From the curtain draped to frame
the old reproductions above him,
to the polished Italian desk,
the day's erasure keeps practicing.

One pigeon rises, then another.
A whole crowd flutters and banks
over the vacant field. The boy
stares at the delicate clock,
fingers the bow, and plays.

Acknowledgments

Thanks to the editors who first published the following pieces, sometimes in different form:

"Box Seats," *Amaranth Review*
"Vacation," *American Literature and Commentary*
"Archeology," *Bellingham Review*
"Hamet, Again," "Screens," and "One Chance," *Boulevard*
"After Sweet Jane," *Café Review*
"Salvaged Wood," "Walk with Salsa," "House of Her," "Catacombs," and "Circus," *Crab Orchard Review*
"County 0," *Laurel Review*
"Body Art," *Luna*
"Mesquite Beans," *Many Mountains Moving*
"Trapdoor" and "The Kingdom," *Notre Dame Review*
"After the Body Deserts," *Parthenon West Review*
"The Street," "Annabel," and "Music Lesson," *Poetry*
"Continental Drift." "Holy Day," and "Saved." *The Prose Poem*
"The Fun," *Quick Fiction*
"Bedtime Story," *Rhino*
"The Cup," *Sentence*
"Thor's Helper," *Southern Poetry Review*
"Fasting," "Chicken," and "The Old Ball Game," *Tampa Review*
"Morning with Lilac" and "Nature," *Third Coast*

About the Author

Barry Silesky's other books include *One Thing That Can Save Us* (prose poems, or short-short fiction, Coffee House Press); *The New Tenants* (verse, Eye of the Comet Press), *Greatest Hits* (verse, Pudding House Press), and the biographies *John Gardner, Literary Outlaw* and *Ferlinghetti: The Artist in His Time*. He edits the literary journal, *ACM* and teaches at Loyola University-Chicago and the School of the Art Institute of Chicago, living next to Wrigley Field with his wife, fiction writer and novelist Sharon Solwitz, and their son, Seth.

About the Book

This Disease is set in Berkeley Oldstyle text types with Copperplate Gothic Titling. The ornament is from the Caravan series by W. A. Dwiggins. The book was designed and typeset by Richard Mathews at the University of Tampa Press. It has been printed on acid-free papers in support of the Green Press Initiative.

Poetry from the University of Tampa Press

Jenny Browne, *At Once*

Richard Chess, *Chair in the Desert*

Richard Chess, *Tekiah*

Jane Ellen Glasser, *Light Persists**

Kathleen Jesme, *Fire Eater*

Lance Larsen, *In All Their Animal Brilliance**

Julia B. Levine, *Ask**

Sarah Maclay, *Whore**

John Willis Menard, *Lays in Summer Lands*

Barry Silesky, *This Disease*

Jordan Smith, *For Appearances**

Jordan Smith, *The Names of Things Are Leaving*

Lisa M. Steinman, *Carslaw's Sequences*

Marjorie Stelmach, *A History of Disappearance*

Richard Terrill, *Coming Late to Rachmaninoff*

Matt Yurdana, *Public Gestures*

* *Denotes winner of the Tampa Review Prize for Poetry*